The Art of War

Interpreted for Content Creators

Strategic Thinking for Building Audience, Influence, and Creative Dominance

ANCIENT WISDOM HACKS

Third Edition

Table of Contents

Part II: Crafting the Plan

- Building Habits and Routines for Consistent Content Creation
- Tools to Avoid Burnout and Maintain Creativity
12. **Measuring Success**
- Key Metrics to Track for Content Creators
- How to Evaluate the Effectiveness of Your Strategy
- Iterating and Improving Based on Data

Conclusion: The Journey Ahead

- Revisiting the Parallels Between *The Art of War* and Content Creation
- Encouragement for Creators to Stay Strategic and Adaptable
- Final Call to Action: Empowering the Reader to Implement the Lessons Learned

Introduction: The Timeless Relevance of Strategy

The Art of War: A Brief Introduction

Few works of literature have endured the test of time as steadfastly as *The Art of War* by Sun Tzu. Written over 2,500 years ago, this ancient Chinese treatise on military strategy is a cornerstone of strategic thinking. Though it was conceived in an era of warlords and dynasties, its principles transcend the battlefield, offering insights into conflict resolution, leadership, and achieving objectives. Sun Tzu's opening lines encapsulate this enduring relevance:

> "The art of war is of vital importance to the state. It is a matter of life and death, a road either to safety or to ruin. Hence it is a subject of inquiry which can on no account be neglected."

For content creators, navigating the digital space mirrors the complexities of ancient warfare. Today's creators contend with ever-changing platforms, fierce competition, and the relentless pursuit of audience engagement. Much like a general commanding troops, a successful creator must master planning, positioning, and adaptability to thrive in this landscape. *The Art of War* serves as a guidebook for this journey, urging creators to view their craft as a strategic endeavor rather than mere content generation.

The Importance of Strategic Thinking for Content Creators

In the digital age, content creation is not just a creative pursuit; it's a strategic endeavor. Each video, blog post, or social media update competes for the attention of a global audience inundated with information. This reality makes strategy an indispensable tool for creators who aim to rise above the noise. Sun Tzu emphasizes the value of foresight and preparation:

> "Victorious warriors win first and then go to war, while defeated warriors go to war first and then seek to win."

This principle underscores the importance of planning in content creation. A viral TikTok or trending blog post often appears spontaneous, but behind the scenes, success is typically the result of meticulous research, deliberate timing, and a clear understanding of the target audience. Without strategy, creators risk wasting their efforts on content that fails to resonate or reach the right audience.

For content creators, strategic thinking bridges the gap between vision and execution. It enables them to identify their niche, craft compelling messages, and deliver those messages effectively. Whether building a personal brand, launching a YouTube channel, or managing a corporate blog, creators who adopt a strategic mindset are better equipped to achieve their goals.

Purpose of the Book: Applying Ancient Wisdom to Modern Digital Strategy

This book seeks to reinterpret the lessons of *The Art of War* for the digital creator. While Sun Tzu wrote about armies and warfare, his principles are universally applicable. Concepts like "knowing the terrain," "using deception," and "seizing opportunities" can be adapted to content creation in profound ways. For instance:

- **Knowing the Terrain** translates to understanding the nuances of platforms like Instagram, YouTube, or TikTok.
- **Using Deception** could involve creating intrigue or curiosity through storytelling and hooks.
- **Seizing Opportunities** encourages creators to capitalize on trends or viral moments.

The goal of this book is not merely to inspire but to provide actionable strategies rooted in Sun Tzu's teachings. By translating these principles into a modern context, creators can gain a competitive edge in the crowded digital space.

The Creator's Battlefield

Defining the Battlefield

The digital landscape is the modern creator's battlefield. Here, instead of armies, there are audiences; instead of fortresses, there are platforms. Each platform—whether it's YouTube, Instagram, TikTok, or LinkedIn—has its unique algorithms, cultures, and constraints. Sun Tzu's wisdom on the importance of terrain resonates powerfully in this context:

"He who knows the terrain and the weather will win.
He who knows neither is destined to lose."

In the content world, "terrain" represents the platforms where creators operate. Each has its rules and strategies for success. For example:

- **YouTube** rewards longer-form, high-quality videos optimized for search.
- **TikTok** emphasizes short, snappy, and entertaining content.
- **Instagram** prioritizes aesthetics and engagement through Stories and Reels.

To thrive, creators must master the nuances of these platforms, tailoring their content and approach accordingly.

Challenges in the Digital Space

The digital space, while rife with opportunities, presents numerous challenges. Content creators often face:

1. **Intense Competition**: The barrier to entry for content creation is low, leading to oversaturation in nearly every niche. Standing out requires a mix of quality, consistency, and strategic differentiation.

   Sun Tzu's advice to "appear where you are not expected" highlights the importance of creativity and innovation in outmaneuvering competitors.

2. **The Attention Economy**: Audiences have limited attention spans and are constantly bombarded with content. Capturing and retaining their attention demands sharp storytelling and relentless value.

3. **Burnout**: The pressure to consistently produce can lead to exhaustion, undermining creativity and productivity. Sun Tzu advises, > "If your forces are not united, it is easy to scatter them," emphasizing the importance of sustainable practices.

Creators must navigate these challenges while maintaining their vision and voice. Strategic planning helps mitigate these risks, ensuring creators can sustain their efforts over time.

Introducing the Main Themes

This book identifies four key themes inspired by *The Art of War* and tailored for content creators: **planning, positioning, adaptability, and execution**.

1. **Planning**: The foundation of any successful endeavor, planning involves setting clear goals, understanding the audience, and developing a roadmap for content creation. Sun Tzu writes:

    "In the midst of chaos, there is also opportunity."

Planning allows creators to identify opportunities and act on them decisively.

2. **Positioning**: Just as Sun Tzu emphasizes the importance of positioning in warfare, creators must carve out a unique space in their niche. This involves branding, storytelling, and crafting a distinct voice that resonates with the audience.

3. **Adaptability**: The digital space evolves rapidly, with platforms constantly updating algorithms and trends shifting overnight. Sun Tzu advises:

"Be extremely subtle, even to the point of formlessness. Be extremely mysterious, even to the point of soundlessness. Thereby you can be the director of the opponent's fate."

Adaptability ensures creators can pivot and thrive amidst change.

4. **Execution**: A brilliant plan is worthless without execution. Sun Tzu states:

"Opportunities multiply as they are seized."

For creators, this means consistently producing and

iterating on content, learning from successes and failures.

Conclusion of the Introduction

The digital age demands more than creativity; it demands strategy. By viewing content creation through the lens of *The Art of War*, creators can master the art of strategic thinking, positioning themselves for sustainable success. This book provides the tools and insights to navigate the creator's battlefield with confidence, turning ancient wisdom into modern triumph.

Chapter 1: Know Yourself

The Importance of Self-Awareness as a Creator

Sun Tzu opens *The Art of War* with a foundational principle that echoes through the ages:

> "If you know the enemy and know yourself, you need not fear the result of a hundred battles."

For creators, the focus here is on the second half of this wisdom: knowing yourself. In the crowded, fast-paced world of content creation, self-awareness is not just an asset—it is a necessity. Without a deep understanding of who you are, what you stand for, and where your strengths lie, you risk becoming lost in a sea of sameness, chasing trends without direction or purpose.

Self-awareness for a creator is about more than just understanding what content you enjoy making. It encompasses knowing:

- Your unique skills and creative strengths.
- Your limitations and areas for growth.
- The values and principles that guide your work.
- The personal goals you want to achieve through content creation.

When creators lack self-awareness, they fall into the trap of imitating others without developing their unique voice or niche.

Sun Tzu warns against this kind of aimless mimicry when he writes:

> "Imitate the enemy until you can achieve their strength, but then seek the terrain where they cannot follow."

For content creators, this means it is okay to draw inspiration from others, but true success comes from defining and embracing your unique identity.

Identifying Your Niche, Voice, and Goals

Finding Your Niche

In *The Art of War*, Sun Tzu emphasizes the importance of occupying the right position:

> "The skillful fighter puts himself into a position which makes defeat impossible and does not miss the moment for defeating the enemy."

For a content creator, this "position" is your niche. Your niche is the focused area or subject matter in which you can excel and provide unique value. Attempting to be everything to everyone dilutes your efforts. Instead, concentrate on a specific topic or field where you can establish authority and connect deeply with your audience.

To identify your niche:

1. Reflect on your passions: What topics excite you? What subjects do you find yourself naturally drawn to?
2. Consider your expertise: What skills or knowledge do you possess that others might find valuable?
3. Research your audience: What are people searching for, and where can you meet a need or solve a problem?

Sun Tzu's advice on terrain reinforces this process. He writes:

> "All warfare is based on deception. Hence, when we are able to attack, we must seem unable; when using our forces, we must appear inactive."

In the context of content creation, this means understanding the competitive landscape. By identifying underserved areas or offering a fresh perspective on popular topics, you can establish a niche that differentiates you from the crowd.

Crafting Your Voice

Your voice is how your audience perceives you—the tone, style, and personality that infuse your content. Sun Tzu's assertion that:

> "Appear at points which the enemy must hasten to defend; march swiftly to places where you are not expected,"

applies here. Your voice should be distinct, unexpected, and memorable. A strong voice builds trust, fosters relatability, and creates a lasting impression.

To develop your voice:

- Reflect on your natural communication style. Are you funny, serious, motivational, or conversational?
- Think about the emotional impact you want your content to have. Do you want to inspire, educate, or entertain?
- Experiment with tone and delivery until you find an authentic fit that resonates with your audience.

Consistency is key. While your content topics may evolve, your voice should remain recognizable and true to your personal brand.

Setting Clear Goals

Sun Tzu writes:

> "When your strategy is deep and far-reaching, what you gain by your calculations will be much."

For content creators, this underscores the importance of setting clear, measurable goals. Without a clear destination, it's easy to become distracted by fleeting trends or short-term gains. Goals provide focus, motivation, and a way to measure progress.

When setting goals, consider:

- **Short-Term Goals**: These might include producing a specific number of videos or growing your follower count by a set percentage within a certain timeframe.
- **Medium-Term Goals**: For example, building a community of engaged followers or diversifying your content offerings.
- **Long-Term Goals**: These could involve launching a business, publishing a book, or achieving a level of influence in your niche.

Effective goals are SMART: Specific, Measurable, Achievable, Relevant, and Time-bound. For instance, instead of saying, "I want to grow my audience," a SMART goal would be, "I want to gain 10,000 followers on Instagram within the next six months by posting three high-quality reels per week."

Practical Exercises to Define Your Content Mission and Vision

Knowing yourself as a creator requires intentional reflection and strategic thinking. Below are practical exercises to help you define your mission and vision.

Exercise 1: The 3-Circle Venn Diagram

Sun Tzu writes:

> "He will win who knows how to handle both superior and inferior forces."

This principle can be applied to understanding the intersection of your passion, expertise, and audience needs. Draw three overlapping circles labeled:

1. What I Love
2. What I Know
3. What My Audience Needs

The overlapping area of these circles represents your "sweet spot"—your niche. This exercise helps clarify where you should focus your efforts.

Exercise 2: The Content Creator's Manifesto

Sun Tzu emphasizes clarity of purpose:

> "The general who wins a battle makes many
> calculations in his temple before the battle is fought."

Write your content creator's manifesto to articulate your mission and vision. Address the following questions:

1. What is the core message I want to share with the world?
2. Who is my ideal audience, and how do I want to impact their lives?
3. How does my content align with my personal values and long-term goals?

Your manifesto serves as a compass, guiding your decisions and keeping you aligned with your purpose.

Exercise 3: SWOT Analysis

Sun Tzu advises:

> "The opportunity of defeating the enemy is provided
> by the enemy himself."

A SWOT analysis helps you assess your strengths, weaknesses, opportunities, and threats as a creator:

- **Strengths**: What are your unique skills and advantages?
- **Weaknesses**: Where do you struggle, and how can you improve?
- **Opportunities**: What trends, tools, or gaps in the market can you leverage?
- **Threats**: What challenges or competitors could hinder your progress?

This analysis enables you to make informed decisions and play to your strengths.

Exercise 4: The Vision Board

Visualization is a powerful tool for achieving clarity and focus. Create a vision board that represents your content goals. Include:

- Images that reflect your ideal brand or aesthetic.
- Quotes that inspire and align with your mission.
- Metrics or milestones you want to achieve.

Place your vision board where you'll see it daily as a reminder of your purpose.

Conclusion

Knowing yourself is the cornerstone of success as a content creator. By understanding your strengths, defining your niche, and setting clear goals, you lay the foundation for a meaningful and impactful journey. As Sun Tzu wisely reminds us:

> "Victorious warriors win first and then go to war, while defeated warriors go to war first and then seek to win."

When you take the time to know yourself, you prepare for victory long before the battle begins. This chapter provides the tools to embark on your content journey with confidence, clarity, and purpose.

Chapter 2: Know Your Audience

Understanding Your Target Audience as Your "Terrain"

In *The Art of War*, Sun Tzu emphasizes the importance of understanding the terrain:

> "If you know the enemy and know yourself, you need not fear the result of a hundred battles. If you know yourself but not the enemy, for every victory gained you will also suffer a defeat. If you know neither the enemy nor yourself, you will succumb in every battle."

For content creators, the "enemy" is not necessarily a competitor; instead, it can be the challenge of winning and retaining your audience's attention. In this analogy, the terrain represents your target audience—their preferences, behaviors, pain points, and expectations. Understanding your audience is akin to mastering the battlefield; it allows you to navigate complexities and seize opportunities effectively.

Your audience is not a monolithic entity; it is composed of individuals with unique needs and desires. By understanding your audience deeply, you can craft content that resonates, builds trust, and fosters loyalty. Sun Tzu's emphasis on tailoring strategies to the terrain directly applies here. He writes:

> "He who knows the terrain and the weather will win."

The "terrain" for creators includes not only the audience's demographics and interests but also the platforms they frequent, the content formats they prefer, and the cultural or emotional triggers that influence their engagement. A creator who ignores this terrain risks producing content that misses the mark, no matter how well-crafted it may be.

Tools and Methods for Audience Research

Understanding your audience requires deliberate effort and the use of reliable tools. Sun Tzu's advice to "plan thoroughly and listen carefully" underscores the value of gathering intelligence before taking action. In the context of content creation, this means investing time in audience research. Below are some of the most effective tools and methods for understanding your audience.

Analytics Tools

Sun Tzu advises:

> "To know your enemy, you must become your enemy."

While not literal, this quote highlights the importance of immersing yourself in the world of your audience to understand them. Analytics tools allow creators to see their content through the audience's eyes, revealing what works, what doesn't, and why.

1. **Google Analytics**: For bloggers and website owners, Google Analytics provides detailed insights into user

behavior. Key metrics include:

- Audience demographics (age, gender, location).
- Pages per session and bounce rates.
- Traffic sources and keywords driving engagement.

2. **Social Media Insights**: Platforms like Instagram, YouTube, and TikTok offer native analytics that reveal:

- Follower demographics.
- Peak engagement times.
- Performance of individual posts or videos.

3. **Third-Party Tools**: Tools like BuzzSumo, SEMrush, and HubSpot allow creators to identify trending topics, analyze competitors, and discover audience preferences.

Using these tools regularly helps creators refine their strategies, ensuring that their content remains relevant and effective.

Surveys and Feedback

Direct input from your audience is invaluable. Sun Tzu emphasizes the importance of listening:

"Opportunities multiply as they are seized."

Surveys and feedback sessions are opportunities to understand your audience's needs, preferences, and pain points directly.

1. **Surveys**: Use tools like Google Forms or SurveyMonkey to create surveys that ask questions such as:

   - What topics do you enjoy most from my content?
   - What challenges are you currently facing in [your niche]?
   - How can I provide more value to you?

2. **Polls and Q&A Sessions**: Platforms like Instagram Stories or YouTube Community posts allow for quick audience polls or open-ended Q&A sessions.

3. **Comment and Message Analysis**: Regularly analyze comments, direct messages, and emails from your audience. These interactions often provide candid insights into what your audience values.

By actively seeking feedback, you demonstrate that you value your audience's opinions, strengthening their connection to your content.

Trend Analysis

Sun Tzu writes:

> "To capture that which you desire, you must act in accordance with the moment."

Keeping up with trends is essential for staying relevant. Trends reflect what your audience is currently interested in, and aligning your content with these trends can significantly boost engagement.

1. **Social Media Listening**: Tools like Hootsuite or Sprout Social allow you to monitor trending topics, hashtags, and conversations within your niche.

2. **Google Trends**: This free tool shows the popularity of search terms over time, helping you identify emerging interests and seasonal patterns.

3. **Competitor Research**: Analyze the content strategies of competitors or similar creators. What trends are they tapping into, and how can you offer a fresh perspective?

4. **Cultural Observations**: Stay attuned to cultural moments, news, and global events that may resonate with your audience.

Trend analysis requires balance. While it's important to capitalize on trends, your content must remain authentic and aligned with your brand's mission.

Building Empathy to Create Content That Resonates

Sun Tzu understood the power of empathy, advising leaders to consider the needs and conditions of their soldiers:

> "Regard your soldiers as your children, and they will follow you into the deepest valleys; look on them as

your own beloved sons, and they will stand by you even unto death."

For content creators, empathy means understanding and respecting the emotions, challenges, and aspirations of your audience. This connection transforms casual viewers into loyal followers and advocates.

The Role of Empathy in Content Creation

1. **Understanding Pain Points**: Every audience has challenges or problems they seek to solve. Whether it's learning a new skill, finding inspiration, or being entertained, empathetic creators identify these needs and address them directly.

2. **Authenticity**: Empathy fosters authenticity. When you genuinely care about your audience, your content reflects that sincerity. Sun Tzu writes:

   "In the midst of chaos, there is also opportunity."

   By showing empathy during moments of uncertainty or challenge, you build deeper connections with your audience.

3. **Tailoring Tone and Messaging**: Empathy guides the tone and messaging of your content. For example, if your

audience is primarily young professionals, your tone might be motivational and practical. If your audience includes parents, your content might focus on relatability and support.

Practical Steps to Build Empathy

1. **Create Personas**: Develop detailed audience personas that represent different segments of your audience. Include:

   - Age, gender, and location.
   - Hobbies and interests.
   - Key challenges and goals.

2. **Engage in Conversations**: Actively participate in discussions within your niche, whether through social media, forums, or live streams. Listening to your audience's thoughts and concerns in real time deepens your understanding.

3. **Storytelling**: Use storytelling to show that you understand your audience's experiences. Share relatable anecdotes, highlight audience success stories, or create content that mirrors their challenges.

4. **Adaptability**: As Sun Tzu advises:

   "Be extremely subtle, even to the point of formlessness."

Empathy allows you to adapt your content to the evolving needs of your audience, ensuring that you remain relevant and engaging.

Conclusion

Understanding your audience is a cornerstone of successful content creation. By viewing your audience as your "terrain" and using tools like analytics, surveys, and trend analysis, you can gain a strategic advantage. More importantly, by building empathy, you foster trust and connection, creating content that not only resonates but also inspires loyalty.

Sun Tzu's timeless wisdom reminds us that the key to victory lies in preparation and understanding. For content creators, knowing your audience is the ultimate preparation—one that paves the way for meaningful, impactful, and sustainable success.

Chapter 3: The Content Landscape

In the vast world of digital content creation, understanding the landscape is paramount. Sun Tzu's wisdom in *The Art of War* provides a powerful lens through which creators can analyze their environment and strategize effectively. He writes:

> "Know the enemy and know yourself, and you can
> fight a hundred battles with no danger of defeat."

For content creators, the "enemy" is not necessarily other creators but the challenges of competition, platform dynamics, and audience engagement. Knowing the content landscape—its opportunities, risks, and key players—allows creators to navigate it effectively, identifying paths to growth and avoiding pitfalls.

This chapter explores three core elements of the content landscape: analyzing the competition, understanding platforms as battlefields, and conducting a SWOT analysis.

Analyzing the Competition

What Works and What Doesn't

In *The Art of War*, Sun Tzu emphasizes the importance of understanding your adversary's strengths and weaknesses:

"The skillful fighter puts himself into a position which makes defeat impossible and does not miss the moment for defeating the enemy."

Analyzing your competition is not about copying their strategies but about learning from their successes and failures. This analysis helps you identify:

1. **What is Effective**: What types of content consistently perform well in your niche? Are there trends or techniques that resonate with the audience?
2. **What is Overdone**: Saturated content formats or topics that no longer hold the audience's attention.
3. **What is Missing**: Gaps in the market where you can provide unique value.

For example, in a niche like fitness content:

- Successful competitors might excel at creating short, high-energy workout videos.
- Overdone content might include generic "Top 10 Tips" lists that fail to engage.
- A potential gap could be personalized advice for people with specific health conditions or limited mobility.

Practical Steps to Analyze Competitors

1. **Identify Key Competitors**: Determine who the leading creators in your niche are. Look for creators who consistently produce high-quality content and engage audiences effectively.

2. **Audit Their Content**: Examine their most successful posts or videos. Analyze factors such as:
   - Format (video, infographic, blog post, etc.).
   - Style (humorous, educational, motivational).
   - Frequency of posting.
   - Engagement levels (comments, shares, likes).
3. **Evaluate Their Weaknesses**: Look for areas where competitors might fall short. For example, a fitness influencer might have great videos but lack interaction with their audience, leaving an opening for you to build a more engaged community.

Sun Tzu advises, > "In conflict, direct confrontation will lead to engagement, but surprise will lead to victory."
 Applying this principle, seek opportunities to differentiate yourself. Surprise your audience with content that competitors aren't delivering.

Case Studies

Analyzing real-world examples can offer valuable insights. Consider:

- **MrBeast (YouTube)**: Known for high-budget challenges and philanthropy-driven content, MrBeast sets himself apart through innovation and reinvestment into his videos. Key takeaway: differentiate through unique value and reinvest resources into audience engagement.
- **Glossier (Instagram)**: This beauty brand thrives by engaging their audience in product development and emphasizing community over hard-sell tactics. Key

takeaway: listen to your audience and involve them in the content creation process.

Understanding Platforms as "Battlefields"

Each content platform represents a unique battlefield with distinct rules, audiences, and engagement strategies. Sun Tzu writes:

> "He who knows the terrain and the weather will win."

For content creators, this "terrain" includes platforms such as YouTube, TikTok, blogs, Instagram, and more. Success depends on tailoring your strategy to the specific dynamics of each platform.

YouTube

YouTube is a long-form content powerhouse, ideal for creators who excel at storytelling, tutorials, or in-depth analysis. Its algorithm rewards watch time, engagement, and consistency. Sun Tzu's guidance is especially relevant here:

> "Opportunities multiply as they are seized."

To succeed on YouTube:

1. Focus on creating content that keeps viewers watching for longer periods.

2. Optimize your videos with SEO-friendly titles, descriptions, and tags.
3. Build momentum by posting consistently and engaging with your audience in comments and live streams.

TikTok

TikTok is a battlefield defined by speed, creativity, and trends. The platform's short-form videos thrive on entertainment, relatability, and quick emotional impact. As Sun Tzu notes:

> "Speed is the essence of war. Take advantage of the enemy's unpreparedness; travel by unexpected routes and strike him where he has taken no precautions."

On TikTok:

- Leverage trends and challenges quickly.
- Use music, humor, and visual storytelling to captivate your audience.
- Experiment with viral hooks in the first few seconds of your videos.

Blogs

Blogging offers a platform for in-depth written content, making it ideal for thought leadership, how-to guides, and evergreen topics.

Sun Tzu's advice to "secure strategic positions" applies to search engine optimization (SEO) here:

> "Those skilled in warfare establish positions that
> cannot be overcome."

Blogging success depends on:

- Researching keywords to ensure your content is discoverable.
- Writing high-quality, comprehensive articles that answer readers' questions.
- Building backlinks and promoting your blog on other platforms.

Instagram

Instagram excels at visual storytelling and fostering community. With a variety of formats (posts, Stories, Reels), the platform allows for diverse strategies. Sun Tzu's emphasis on adaptability resonates here:

> "Be extremely subtle, even to the point of
> formlessness. Be extremely mysterious, even to the
> point of soundlessness."

To succeed on Instagram:

1. Mix static posts with dynamic content like Reels or Stories.
2. Use hashtags strategically to reach new audiences.

3. Build community through direct engagement (comments, polls, and Q&A sessions).

LinkedIn

For professional networking and thought leadership, LinkedIn provides an unparalleled opportunity. Sun Tzu advises:

> "He who knows when he can fight and when he cannot will be victorious."

On LinkedIn, success often hinges on credibility and consistency. Share actionable insights, engage with industry trends, and connect with professionals in your field.

SWOT Analysis for Content Creators

A SWOT (Strengths, Weaknesses, Opportunities, Threats) analysis is a critical tool for assessing your position in the content landscape. Sun Tzu's strategic philosophy supports this approach:

> "Ponder and deliberate before you make a move."

By identifying your internal strengths and weaknesses alongside external opportunities and threats, you can make informed decisions and craft a robust content strategy.

Strengths

Your strengths are the unique qualities and assets that give you an advantage over others. These might include:

- Exceptional storytelling skills.
- A distinctive voice or perspective.
- Access to high-quality equipment or resources.

Sun Tzu writes:

> "The victorious army is first victorious and then seeks battle."

In content creation, this means leaning into your strengths to build a solid foundation before competing for audience attention.

Weaknesses

Weaknesses are internal factors that may hinder your success, such as:

- Lack of consistency in posting.
- Limited understanding of a platform's algorithm.
- Weak branding or unclear messaging.

Sun Tzu advises:

> "Do not engage an enemy more powerful than you.
> And if you do engage, be prepared to retreat."

Address weaknesses proactively. For instance, if your visuals are poor, invest in better equipment or training. If you struggle with consistency, create a manageable content calendar.

Opportunities

Opportunities are external factors you can leverage to your advantage. These might include:

- Emerging trends or untapped niches.
- Platform updates or new features.
- Collaboration with other creators.

Sun Tzu's insight on opportunities is particularly apt:

> "In the midst of chaos, there is also opportunity."

Stay vigilant for changes in the content landscape that you can capitalize on. For example, when TikTok introduced the "duet" feature, creators who adapted quickly saw significant growth.

Threats

Threats are external factors that could negatively impact your success, such as:

- Increasing competition in your niche.
- Algorithm changes that reduce your visibility.
- Audience preferences shifting away from your content style.

Sun Tzu writes:

> "Move not unless you see an advantage; use not your troops unless there is something to be gained."

Mitigate threats by diversifying your content, staying adaptable, and continuously engaging with your audience to understand their evolving needs.

Conclusion

Understanding the content landscape is crucial for success as a creator. By analyzing competitors, tailoring strategies to platform dynamics, and conducting a SWOT analysis, you can position yourself effectively for growth. As Sun Tzu wisely observes:

> "The whole secret lies in confusing the enemy, so that he cannot fathom our real intent."

In content creation, this means remaining unpredictable, innovative, and always aligned with your audience's needs. With a deep understanding of the landscape, you can navigate challenges and seize opportunities, paving the way for sustained success in your content journey.

Chapter 4: Planning for Victory

Sun Tzu begins *The Art of War* with a profound declaration about the importance of planning:

> "The art of war is of vital importance to the state. It is a matter of life and death, a road either to safety or to ruin."

For content creators, planning serves as the difference between aimless content production and sustained success. Much like a military commander designs a strategy to win battles, a creator must plan meticulously to achieve their goals in the crowded and competitive digital landscape. This chapter explores how to craft a content calendar as a campaign plan, balance long-term goals with short-term tactics, and leverage tools for efficient content planning.

Crafting a Content Calendar as a "Campaign Plan"

Sun Tzu emphasizes the importance of preparation in warfare:

> "Victorious warriors win first and then go to war, while defeated warriors go to war first and then seek to win."

A content calendar is the creator's equivalent of a campaign plan—a detailed roadmap that outlines what content to create, when to publish it, and how to promote it. It ensures consistency, minimizes stress, and allows creators to seize opportunities effectively.

Why a Content Calendar Matters

1. **Consistency**: Platforms reward creators who post regularly. A content calendar helps maintain a steady flow of content, ensuring you stay relevant to your audience.
2. **Organization**: It simplifies the complexity of managing multiple ideas, platforms, and formats.
3. **Strategy Alignment**: A calendar ensures your daily activities align with larger goals, whether it's growing your audience or launching a product.
4. **Adaptability**: A well-structured calendar allows for flexibility, enabling creators to incorporate trends or respond to unexpected opportunities.

Steps to Build a Content Calendar

1. **Define Your Goals** Begin by asking: What do you hope to achieve? Sun Tzu advises:

   "The general who wins a battle makes many calculations in his temple before the battle is fought."

   Goals can include increasing follower counts, boosting engagement, or driving sales. Clearly defined objectives serve as the foundation of your calendar.

2. **Identify Key Themes and Topics** Break down your goals into themes that guide your content. For example, a fitness creator might focus on themes like strength training, nutrition, and mental wellness. Align these themes with your audience's interests and needs.

3. **Set Publishing Frequency** Determine how often you can realistically publish without sacrificing quality. As Sun Tzu notes:

"The wise warrior avoids the battle that cannot be won."

Be realistic about your capacity to create content consistently.

4. **Choose Content Types and Formats** Match your content formats to your platform and audience preferences. Examples include:

   - Blog posts for thought leadership.
   - Videos or Reels for high engagement on platforms like TikTok or Instagram.
   - Infographics for quick, shareable insights.

5. **Assign Deadlines** Assign specific publishing dates to each piece of content. Deadlines create accountability and ensure you stay on track.

6. **Plan Promotion Strategies** Incorporate steps for promoting your content, such as:

   - Sharing on social media.
   - Collaborating with other creators.
   - Repurposing content across multiple platforms.
7. **Review and Adjust** Regularly review your calendar's performance. Sun Tzu writes:

   "Opportunities multiply as they are seized."

   Use analytics to identify what works and refine your approach.

Balancing Long-Term Goals with Short-Term Tactics

Sun Tzu teaches the importance of balancing strategy and tactics:

"Strategy without tactics is the slowest route to victory. Tactics without strategy is the noise before defeat."

In content creation, long-term goals represent the overarching vision (e.g., becoming an authority in your niche), while short-term tactics are the day-to-day actions that move you toward those goals.

Defining Long-Term Goals

Long-term goals should reflect your mission as a creator.
Examples include:

- Building a personal brand as a thought leader.
- Creating a sustainable income stream from your content.
- Growing a community of engaged followers.

Sun Tzu writes:

> "The victorious strategist only seeks battle after the
> victory has been won."

Plan your content with these ultimate objectives in mind. For
instance, if your goal is to launch an online course in six months,
your content strategy should focus on building credibility in that
area.

Executing Short-Term Tactics

Short-term tactics include the actions you take to achieve your
immediate objectives, such as:

- Posting a daily TikTok to boost engagement.
- Running a poll to gather audience insights.
- Creating a blog series on trending topics.

These tactics must align with your long-term vision. For example, creating viral TikToks might be fun, but if they don't attract your target audience, they won't contribute to your broader goals.

Sun Tzu reminds us:

> "Do not repeat the tactics which have gained you one victory, but let your methods be regulated by the infinite variety of circumstances."

Tactics should remain adaptable, allowing you to pivot based on performance and audience feedback.

Tools for Efficient Content Planning

Planning content manually can be overwhelming, especially for creators managing multiple platforms. Thankfully, a variety of tools are available to streamline the process. Sun Tzu's emphasis on preparation applies here:

> "In the midst of chaos, there is also opportunity."

By using the right tools, creators can turn chaos into opportunity, saving time and improving efficiency.

Content Management Tools

1. **Trello or Asana**: These project management tools help creators organize their content calendars, assign tasks,

and track deadlines.

  - ○ Example: Use Trello boards to organize content by stages (e.g., ideation, drafting, publishing).
2. **Notion**: A highly customizable workspace for managing notes, calendars, and content schedules in one place.

  - ○ Example: Create a template for tracking ideas, publishing dates, and analytics.

Social Media Scheduling Tools

1. **Buffer**: Allows creators to schedule posts across multiple platforms, analyze engagement, and optimize posting times.
2. **Hootsuite**: A robust platform for managing, scheduling, and monitoring social media campaigns.
3. **Later**: Specializes in visual platforms like Instagram and Pinterest, offering features for planning and previewing posts.

SEO and Keyword Research Tools

1. **Google Trends**: Identifies trending topics to incorporate into your content calendar.
2. **SEMrush**: Provides detailed keyword research and competitor analysis for blogs and YouTube videos.
3. **AnswerThePublic**: Offers insights into common questions and topics your audience is searching for.

Analytics Tools

1. **Google Analytics**: Tracks website traffic and audience behavior.
2. **Platform-Specific Insights**: Use Instagram Insights, YouTube Studio, or TikTok Analytics to understand what content resonates.

Collaboration Tools

1. **Slack**: Facilitates communication between team members or collaborators.
2. **Google Drive**: Stores and shares drafts, images, and videos for easy collaboration.

Conclusion

Planning for victory as a content creator requires foresight, organization, and adaptability. A well-crafted content calendar serves as a campaign plan, ensuring consistency and focus. By balancing long-term goals with short-term tactics and leveraging the right tools, creators can position themselves for sustained success.

Sun Tzu's wisdom resonates deeply in this process:

> "The supreme art of war is to subdue the enemy
> without fighting."

For content creators, victory comes not from outspending or outposting competitors but from outthinking them. With a strategic plan in place, creators can navigate the digital landscape confidently, turning their vision into reality while staying flexible enough to seize new opportunities.

Chapter 5: Positioning for Success

Sun Tzu's *The Art of War* is a masterclass in positioning—establishing yourself in the right place, at the right time, with the right strategy to achieve victory. He writes:

> "Position yourself where you cannot lose, and you will defeat even the most powerful enemy."

In the world of content creation, positioning is the key to success. It involves defining your brand, identifying what sets you apart, and building a strong identity that resonates with your audience. Without clear positioning, even the most creative and engaging content can be lost in a saturated market.

This chapter explores the importance of branding, case studies of successful creators who mastered positioning, and actionable strategies to differentiate yourself in a competitive landscape.

The Importance of Branding in Establishing Your Position

Branding is the foundation of your position as a content creator. It is the perception your audience forms about you—your values, voice, visual identity, and the unique promise you deliver. Sun Tzu highlights the importance of building strength in a position:

"The skillful fighter cultivates strength and avoids weaknesses."

For creators, branding is that cultivated strength. A strong brand conveys credibility, builds trust, and creates an emotional connection with your audience. It ensures that you remain recognizable and memorable, even in a crowded field.

Elements of a Strong Brand

1. **Mission and Vision** Your mission defines what you stand for, while your vision represents what you aspire to achieve. Together, they provide clarity and purpose. As Sun Tzu advises:

   "The general who advances without coveting fame and retreats without fearing disgrace, whose only thought is to protect his country and do good service for his sovereign, is the jewel of the kingdom."

   A mission-driven creator focuses on delivering value to their audience, not merely chasing trends or vanity metrics.

2. **Voice and Personality** Your voice is the tone and style of your communication, while your personality is the unique character you bring to your content. Consistency in these elements helps establish familiarity and trust.

3. **Visual Identity** From your logo to your color palette, visual branding plays a crucial role in positioning. Think of it as

your "armor" on the battlefield—it makes you recognizable and distinct.

4. **Value Proposition** Your value proposition answers the question: "Why should people follow me instead of someone else?" It is the unique benefit or perspective you bring to your niche.

Building a Personal or Brand Identity

To establish a strong position, creators must first identify their unique identity. Sun Tzu's focus on understanding one's strengths and weaknesses applies here:

"Know yourself and you will win all battles."

Begin by reflecting on the following:

- **What makes you unique?** Identify your strengths, passions, and experiences that set you apart.
- **Who is your audience?** Understand the needs, desires, and pain points of your ideal followers.
- **What is your message?** Clarify the core themes or values you want your content to communicate.

Case Studies: Successful Creators and Their Unique Positioning

Great content creators understand the power of positioning. They carve out niches, establish clear identities, and consistently deliver value. Let's explore a few examples of successful creators who have mastered the art of positioning.

1. Marie Kondo (Tidying and Minimalism)

Marie Kondo built her brand around the concept of "sparking joy" through tidying. Her unique positioning as an organizational expert with a minimalist philosophy resonated globally, culminating in best-selling books and a Netflix series. Kondo's success lies in:

- A clear and memorable message: "Does it spark joy?"
- Consistent branding: Her visuals, tone, and presentation reflect simplicity and calmness.
- Niche expertise: By focusing solely on decluttering and organization, she dominated her field.

Sun Tzu's emphasis on focus aligns with Kondo's strategy:

> "He who tries to defend everything defends nothing."

By narrowing her scope, Kondo avoided dilution and became a household name in her niche.

2. MrBeast (Entertainment and Philanthropy)

MrBeast, one of YouTube's most influential creators, stands out for his blend of high-stakes entertainment and philanthropy. His unique positioning includes:

- **Creative Concepts**: Videos that are larger-than-life, such as "I Bought Everything in a Store."
- **Purpose-Driven Content**: Generous donations and charity projects, which build goodwill.
- **Consistency and Reinvestment**: MrBeast reinvests revenue into bigger and better videos, creating a cycle of growth.

His strategy reflects Sun Tzu's principle:

> "The clever combatant imposes his will on the enemy but does not allow the enemy's will to be imposed on him."

By defining his niche so distinctly, MrBeast avoids being boxed in by competitors or trends.

---

3. Glossier (Beauty and Community)

Glossier disrupted the beauty industry by positioning itself as a community-driven brand. Instead of dictating beauty standards, it focused on empowering its customers to define their own. Glossier's success stems from:

- **User-Generated Content**: Encouraging customers to share their experiences.
- **Relatable Branding**: Simple, approachable visuals and messaging.
- **Focus on Community**: Building a loyal fan base through interaction and inclusivity.

Sun Tzu's philosophy of understanding the terrain resonates with Glossier's strategy:

> "The general who thoroughly understands the advantages of varying conditions knows how to handle his troops."

By recognizing the shift toward inclusivity and authenticity in beauty, Glossier positioned itself as a leader in this movement.

How to Differentiate Yourself in a Saturated Market

In a crowded content landscape, differentiation is critical. Sun Tzu writes:

> "Appear at points which the enemy must hasten to defend; march swiftly to places where you are not expected."

This principle highlights the importance of finding and exploiting gaps in the market. Here are actionable steps to differentiate yourself.

1. Define Your Niche

A niche provides focus and clarity. Instead of trying to appeal to everyone, identify a specific audience or subject area where you can excel. Consider:

- **Micro-Niches**: In a competitive space, drill down into a more specific sub-niche. For example, instead of general fitness, focus on "yoga for seniors" or "home workouts for busy professionals."
- **Audience Gaps**: Look for underserved communities or overlooked topics in your field.

---

2. Offer Unique Value

Differentiate by delivering value that others don't. This could include:

- **Expertise**: Share insights or skills that are rare in your niche.
- **Innovation**: Experiment with new formats, such as interactive content or gamified experiences.
- **Personal Stories**: Use your background, struggles, or journey to create a relatable narrative.

Sun Tzu's wisdom on adapting to opportunities applies here:

> "In the midst of chaos, there is also opportunity."

---

3. Cultivate Authenticity

Authenticity is a powerful differentiator. Audiences gravitate toward creators who are genuine and relatable. To cultivate authenticity:

- Share your behind-the-scenes process or personal experiences.
- Acknowledge your imperfections; audiences appreciate vulnerability.
- Stay true to your values, even when trends tempt you to stray.

Sun Tzu emphasizes the value of honesty:

> "All warfare is based on deception. But in times of peace, build your reputation on trust."

---

4. Experiment with Formats and Platforms

Standing out often requires being the first or the best at something new. Experiment with:

- **Emerging Platforms**: Early adopters of platforms like TikTok or Clubhouse gained massive followings by capitalizing on low competition.
- **Innovative Formats**: Try formats your competitors aren't using, such as live streams, VR content, or interactive videos.

5. Build Strong Relationships

Differentiate yourself by cultivating deeper connections with your audience:

- Respond to comments and messages.
- Create opportunities for interaction, such as Q&A sessions or polls.
- Foster a sense of community through memberships or exclusive content.

Sun Tzu writes:

> "Treat your soldiers as your own beloved children,
> and they will follow you into the deepest valleys."

For content creators, treating your audience with care and respect fosters loyalty and trust.

Conclusion

Positioning is the cornerstone of success in content creation. By establishing a strong brand, learning from successful examples, and differentiating yourself in a saturated market, you can carve out a unique place in your niche. Sun Tzu's wisdom resonates throughout this journey:

> "Victory usually goes to the army who has
> better-trained officers and men."

For creators, "training" involves refining your voice, understanding your audience, and staying ahead of trends. With a clear position and purpose, you can rise above the competition and build a lasting legacy in the digital space.

Chapter 6: Timing is Everything

Sun Tzu's *The Art of War* repeatedly emphasizes the importance of timing in achieving victory:

> "The successful fighter is one who understands the right moment and seizes it, striking where the enemy is unprepared."

In the realm of content creation, timing plays an equally crucial role. Delivering the right content at the right time can significantly amplify its impact, whether it's riding a viral trend, aligning with seasonal moments, or consistently publishing when your audience is most engaged. This chapter explores the art of timing, the tools to perfect your timing strategy, and how to balance urgency with quality.

The Art of Timing Your Content

Understanding Trends

In the fast-paced digital landscape, trends are fleeting yet powerful opportunities to amplify your content's reach. As Sun Tzu advises:

> "Opportunities multiply as they are seized."

Trends reflect what the audience is currently interested in, making them a strategic entry point to gain visibility and relevance.

Examples of trends include viral hashtags on Twitter, challenges on TikTok, or breaking news stories relevant to your niche.

How to Leverage Trends

1. **Act Quickly**: Timing is critical when capitalizing on trends. The earlier you participate, the more visibility you gain.
2. **Maintain Authenticity**: Ensure the trend aligns with your brand and messaging. Jumping on a trend that feels forced can alienate your audience.
3. **Add Value**: Instead of merely imitating the trend, offer a fresh perspective or unique twist that aligns with your expertise.

Sun Tzu's principle of adaptability underscores this approach:

> "Just as water adapts to the shape of the ground, a warrior must adapt to the enemy."

Creators who adapt swiftly and thoughtfully to trends can capture their audience's attention while staying true to their identity.

Virality: The Unpredictable Timing

Virality is often seen as the holy grail of content creation. However, going viral is as much about timing as it is about creativity. Viral content usually emerges when it aligns perfectly with the cultural zeitgeist, audience emotions, and platform dynamics. Sun Tzu's observation about the chaotic nature of opportunity applies here:

> "In the midst of chaos, there is also opportunity."

Characteristics of Viral Content

- **Relatability**: Content that taps into universal emotions or shared experiences has a higher chance of going viral.
- **Timeliness**: Viral content often resonates with current events or cultural moments.
- **Shareability**: Content that is easy to share, whether through humor, inspiration, or intrigue, spreads faster.

Creators can improve their chances of going viral by staying tuned to what's trending and delivering content that is both timely and shareable.

Consistency: The Foundation of Timing

While trends and virality offer bursts of visibility, consistency is the backbone of long-term success. Sun Tzu's focus on steady preparation aligns with the importance of consistency:

> "He will win who has prepared himself and waits to take the enemy unprepared."

For content creators, consistency means showing up regularly for your audience. Platforms reward consistent posting with better visibility, and audiences come to rely on your regular presence. The key to consistency lies in creating a sustainable schedule and sticking to it.

Best Practices for Consistency

1. **Set a Realistic Schedule**: Choose a posting frequency that you can maintain without compromising quality.

2. **Batch Create Content**: To stay ahead, create multiple pieces of content in advance.
3. **Plan Around Your Audience's Habits**: Post when your audience is most active to maximize engagement.

Tools for Identifying the Best Times to Post and Engage

Sun Tzu emphasizes the importance of strategic intelligence:

> "Know the enemy and know yourself, and you can
> fight a hundred battles with no danger of defeat."

In content creation, this intelligence comes from understanding your audience's behavior, which can be achieved through analytics tools. These tools provide insights into when your audience is most active and engaged, allowing you to optimize your timing.

Platform-Specific Tools

1. **Instagram Insights**

   - Provides data on follower activity, including the days and hours they are most active.
   - Helps identify which types of posts perform best at specific times.

2. **YouTube Analytics**

   - Offers insights into when your subscribers are online.

- Tracks video watch time and engagement to inform optimal posting times.

3. **TikTok Analytics**

   - Shows audience activity trends and performance metrics for videos.
   - Useful for tracking the best times to post short-form content.

4. **Facebook Analytics**

   - Highlights engagement patterns and audience demographics.
   - Identifies the best times to post based on historical performance.

Third-Party Scheduling and Analytics Tools

1. **Hootsuite**

   - Allows creators to schedule posts across multiple platforms.
   - Analyzes historical performance to suggest optimal posting times.

2. **Buffer**

   - Tracks engagement metrics and recommends the best times to publish content.
   - Offers an intuitive calendar for scheduling.

3. **Sprout Social**

- Provides detailed audience insights and competitor analysis.
- Identifies high-performing time slots for engagement.

4. **Later**

- Specializes in visual platforms like Instagram and Pinterest.
- Includes a feature to auto-schedule posts during peak engagement periods.

Using these tools ensures that your content reaches the maximum number of people at the right time, enhancing its impact and engagement.

Balancing Urgency with Quality

Sun Tzu warns against rushing into battle without preparation:

> "He will win who knows when to fight and when not to fight."

In content creation, this wisdom translates to balancing the need for timely content with maintaining high standards of quality. Rushed, low-quality content can harm your reputation, while excessive perfectionism can cause you to miss key opportunities.

When to Prioritize Urgency

1. **Trends and Breaking News**
   - Strike while the iron is hot. For example, if a trending hashtag aligns with your niche, prioritize speed over perfection to ride the wave of engagement.
2. **Seasonal Opportunities**
   - Time-sensitive content, such as holiday campaigns or event-related posts, requires quick execution.

When to Focus on Quality

1. **Evergreen Content**
   - Posts or videos that remain relevant over time should prioritize depth and accuracy. For example, a comprehensive tutorial or a thought-leadership piece.
2. **Signature Projects**
   - High-stakes content, such as product launches or collaborations, demands meticulous planning and execution.

Striking the Right Balance

1. **Use Templates and Frameworks**
   - Create reusable templates for graphics, captions, or videos to streamline production without sacrificing quality.

2. **Set Clear Priorities**
    - Assess each piece of content based on urgency and importance. If something is both time-sensitive and high-quality, allocate extra resources to ensure its success.
3. **Learn from Analytics**
    - Track performance to refine your balance between urgency and quality. Sun Tzu's advice to "ponder and deliberate" before action applies here.

Case Study: Timing in Action

Example: Oreo's "Dunk in the Dark" Tweet

During the 2013 Super Bowl, a power outage occurred, and Oreo's marketing team responded with a perfectly timed tweet: "You can still dunk in the dark." The simple yet relevant message went viral, demonstrating the power of agility and timing.

> Sun Tzu: "Speed is the essence of war."

Oreo's quick response capitalized on a cultural moment, showcasing how timing can amplify a brand's reach.

Conclusion

Timing is a critical factor in content creation, influencing whether your work gets noticed or overlooked. By mastering the art of timing, using analytics tools to optimize posting schedules, and balancing urgency with quality, creators can maximize their impact and engagement.

Sun Tzu's timeless wisdom encapsulates the essence of this chapter:

> "Take advantage of the enemy's unpreparedness;
> travel by unexpected routes and strike him where he
> has taken no precautions."

For content creators, success often lies in seizing the right moment and delivering content that aligns perfectly with audience expectations and cultural currents. With thoughtful timing, you can amplify your reach, build stronger connections with your audience, and achieve sustained growth in your content journey.

Chapter 7: Adaptability and Pivots

Sun Tzu's *The Art of War* reminds us of a crucial lesson for success in any endeavor:

> "In the midst of chaos, there is also opportunity."

In the world of content creation, chaos is an inevitable part of the digital landscape. Platforms evolve, algorithms change, audience preferences shift, and what worked yesterday may no longer work tomorrow. Success in this space requires not only creativity but also adaptability—the ability to recognize and respond to change effectively.

This chapter explores the inevitability of change in digital platforms, the signs that indicate it's time to pivot your strategy, and inspiring examples of creators who thrived by adapting to new circumstances.

The Inevitability of Change in Digital Platforms

In the dynamic world of content creation, the only constant is change. Sun Tzu's teachings emphasize the need to anticipate and prepare for evolving conditions:

> "The nature of war is constant change. What remains unchanging is the need to adapt."

How Platforms Evolve

1. **Algorithm Updates** Platforms like YouTube, Instagram, TikTok, and Facebook frequently update their algorithms. These changes can affect how content is ranked, discovered, and distributed. For example:

    - Instagram's shift from chronological feeds to engagement-based algorithms significantly altered how posts reach audiences.
    - YouTube's focus on watch time and viewer retention has forced creators to prioritize longer, engaging videos.

2. **New Features** Platforms often introduce new features to keep users engaged, such as TikTok's "duet" feature or Instagram's Reels. Creators who adopt these features early often gain a competitive advantage.

3. **Shifting User Preferences** Audiences continually evolve in how they consume content. For instance:

    - The rise of short-form content (e.g., TikTok) has changed how creators approach storytelling.
    - Increasing demand for authenticity has driven more creators to adopt unpolished, raw styles over highly curated content.

Navigating Platform Changes

Sun Tzu advises:

> "He who knows when he can fight and when he cannot will be victorious."

Creators must learn to discern when to double down on their current strategies and when to adapt. Failing to evolve with platform changes can lead to stagnation, reduced visibility, and a loss of audience trust.

Signs It's Time to Pivot Your Strategy or Content Focus

Knowing when to pivot is a critical skill for content creators. As Sun Tzu notes:

> "If circumstances change, act accordingly."

Here are some common signs that it may be time to adjust your strategy or content focus:

---

1. Declining Engagement

If your likes, comments, views, or shares are consistently declining, it's a clear signal that your current approach is no longer resonating with your audience. Analyze your metrics to identify patterns and areas for improvement.

Example:

- A travel blogger might notice a drop in engagement on long-form blogs and pivot to creating shorter, destination-specific Instagram Reels that align with audience preferences.

2. Platform Evolution

When a platform introduces significant changes, such as algorithm updates or new features, it's time to reassess your strategy. Ignoring these shifts can make your content less visible.

Example:

- When Instagram introduced Reels to compete with TikTok, many creators who embraced the feature early saw significant growth in reach and engagement.

3. Shifts in Audience Behavior

Pay attention to changes in how your audience interacts with your content. Are they asking for different topics? Are their consumption habits changing? Sun Tzu highlights the importance of understanding the terrain:

> "Adapt your methods to the terrain, and you will always succeed."

Listening to your audience ensures your content remains relevant.

4. Personal Burnout or Loss of Passion

If you find yourself losing enthusiasm for your current content focus, it may be time to pivot. Creating content that aligns with your evolving interests not only keeps you motivated but also attracts an audience that resonates with your authenticity.

Example:

- A fitness influencer burned out from posting only workouts could pivot to wellness content, sharing insights on mental health, nutrition, and self-care.

---

5. New Opportunities or Trends

Sometimes, a new trend or opportunity emerges that aligns with your brand or interests. Pivoting to seize these moments can reinvigorate your content strategy. Sun Tzu writes:

> "Opportunities multiply as they are seized."

Examples of Creators Who Thrived by Adapting to Change

History is filled with creators who successfully pivoted their strategies to thrive in changing environments. Their stories demonstrate the power of adaptability in overcoming challenges and seizing new opportunities.

---

1. Casey Neistat: From Filmmaker to YouTube Vlogger

Casey Neistat, a filmmaker known for his innovative storytelling, initially built his career in traditional media. However, he pivoted to YouTube when he recognized the platform's potential for creative independence and direct audience engagement. By embracing vlogging and crafting visually stunning daily videos, he redefined the genre and grew a massive following.

Key Lesson:

Neistat's willingness to shift from traditional filmmaking to digital content exemplifies Sun Tzu's advice:

> "Appear at points which the enemy must hasten to defend; march swiftly to places where you are not expected."

By moving into the uncharted territory of high-quality vlogs, Neistat positioned himself as a pioneer.

---

2. Jenna Marbles: Evolving with Authenticity

Jenna Marbles started on YouTube with comedic videos that resonated with a broad audience. Over time, she adapted her content to align with her evolving interests and values, exploring topics like DIY projects and personal growth. Her authentic approach allowed her to maintain relevance and build a loyal fan base for over a decade.

Key Lesson:

Sun Tzu writes:

> "Regard your soldiers as your children, and they will
> follow you into the deepest valleys."

Jenna's genuine connection with her audience fostered loyalty,
enabling her to pivot successfully without losing her core fans.

---

3. TikTok Stars Embracing Multi-Platform Strategies

Many TikTok creators who found initial fame on the platform have
expanded to YouTube, Instagram, and other platforms to diversify
their reach and income streams. For example, Charli D'Amelio
transitioned from dance videos on TikTok to launching a
family-focused reality show and brand partnerships.

Key Lesson:

Sun Tzu advises:

> "The wise warrior moves where he is certain of victory
> and prepares for any terrain."

Diversifying platforms allows creators to protect themselves
against algorithm changes or the decline of a single platform.

---

4. Marques Brownlee: Adapting to Tech Trends

Marques Brownlee (MKBHD) began his YouTube career reviewing consumer electronics. Over time, he adapted his content to cover broader tech trends, including electric vehicles, cutting-edge gadgets, and interviews with industry leaders. This evolution allowed him to stay relevant as the tech landscape changed.

Key Lesson:

Sun Tzu's principle of observing and adapting aligns with Marques's strategy:

> "Those who are skilled in combat do not become angered, and those who are skilled at winning do not become afraid. Thus, the wise win before the fight, while the ignorant fight to win."

By staying ahead of trends, Marques ensured his continued growth and influence.

Strategies for Successful Adaptation

Adaptation requires a mix of strategic thinking, creativity, and audience awareness. Here's how creators can pivot effectively:

1. Monitor Analytics and Feedback

Sun Tzu writes:

> "Ponder and deliberate before you make a move."

Regularly analyze your performance metrics and audience feedback to identify areas that need adjustment. Tools like YouTube Analytics, Instagram Insights, and Google Analytics can provide valuable data.

2. Experiment with New Formats

Test different content formats to see what resonates with your audience. For example:

- If long-form blogs are losing traction, try creating short-form social media posts.
- Experiment with video content if your current strategy is text-heavy.

3. Embrace Trends Early

Stay informed about emerging trends in your niche. Use tools like Google Trends, BuzzSumo, and TikTok's Discover page to identify opportunities.

4. Stay True to Your Brand

While adaptation is essential, ensure that your pivots align with your brand values and messaging. Sudden, drastic shifts may confuse or alienate your audience.

5. Seek Inspiration from Others

Learn from creators in your field who have successfully adapted. Study their strategies and consider how similar approaches could work for you.

Conclusion

Adaptability is not just a survival skill—it's a competitive advantage in the ever-changing digital landscape. By recognizing the inevitability of change, identifying the right moments to pivot, and drawing inspiration from others who have thrived, creators can stay ahead of the curve.

Sun Tzu's wisdom encapsulates the essence of this chapter:

> "The supreme art of war is to subdue the enemy
> without fighting."

For content creators, the "enemy" is stagnation, irrelevance, or resistance to change. By embracing adaptability and viewing change as an opportunity rather than a threat, creators can chart a path to sustained success, no matter how the digital terrain evolves.

Chapter 8: Content as a Weapon

In *The Art of War*, Sun Tzu frequently emphasizes the importance of weaponry and the skillful use of resources:

> "Weapons are tools of ill omen to be used only when there is no choice. To rely on them for every conflict is not the mark of a wise leader."

For content creators, the content itself is the weapon of choice. Skillfully wielded, it can captivate audiences, educate followers, inspire action, and establish authority. However, just as a general must select the appropriate weapon for a specific battle, a content creator must carefully choose the type, format, and delivery method of their material to achieve the desired result.

This chapter explores the different types of content, their strategic applications, the importance of aligning content formats with your goals, and how to repurpose content for maximum impact.

Types of Content and Their Uses

1. Educational Content

Sun Tzu states:

> "He who is prudent and lies in wait for an enemy who is not, will be victorious."

Educational content allows creators to position themselves as experts in their field, arming their audience with knowledge and practical solutions. It is particularly effective for building trust and loyalty over time, as audiences consistently return to creators who offer value.

Examples of Educational Content

- **How-To Guides**: Blog posts or videos that teach step-by-step processes (e.g., "How to Edit Videos Like a Pro").
- **Tutorials**: Detailed demonstrations on using specific tools or techniques (e.g., Photoshop tutorials).
- **Webinars**: Live or recorded sessions that provide in-depth insights into a topic.

Strategic Uses

- Attracts an audience actively seeking solutions.
- Builds credibility and positions you as an authority in your niche.
- Encourages repeat visits as audiences view you as a reliable resource.

---

2. Entertaining Content

Sun Tzu observes:

> "The skillful fighter puts himself beyond the possibility of defeat by creating diversions."

Entertainment is a powerful diversion—it captures attention, sparks emotion, and encourages sharing. Entertaining content thrives on relatability, humor, and storytelling, making it highly shareable and effective for rapid audience growth.

Examples of Entertaining Content

- **Humorous Videos**: Skits, memes, or parodies that resonate with your audience.
- **Storytelling**: Sharing personal experiences or fictional tales that connect emotionally.
- **Challenges**: Fun, participatory activities (e.g., TikTok dance trends or viral dares).

Strategic Uses

- Builds emotional connections with your audience.
- Drives social sharing, leading to broader reach and exposure.
- Humanizes your brand, making it more relatable and engaging.

---

3. Engaging Content

Sun Tzu writes:

> "Engage people with what they expect; it is what they are able to discern and confirms their projections. It settles them into predictable patterns of response, occupying their minds while you wait for the extraordinary moment."

Engaging content invites direct interaction, fostering a sense of community and deepening relationships with your audience. It shifts the focus from broadcasting to facilitating dialogue.

Examples of Engaging Content

- **Polls and Surveys**: Interactive posts that invite opinions (e.g., "What's your favorite workout playlist?").
- **Live Q&A Sessions**: Real-time interactions with followers to answer their questions.
- **Contests and Giveaways**: Incentivized activities that encourage participation (e.g., "Tag a friend to win!").

Strategic Uses

- Increases follower interaction and strengthens community bonds.
- Provides valuable audience insights and feedback.
- Boosts platform algorithms that reward high engagement.

Matching Content Formats to Your Strategy

Sun Tzu reminds us:

"Every battle is won or lost before it is ever fought."

Success in content creation begins with choosing the right format to align with your goals, audience preferences, and platform dynamics. Each format has strengths and limitations, and the choice depends on your strategic objectives.

1. Videos

Video is the most versatile and engaging format, with platforms like YouTube, TikTok, and Instagram Reels driving its dominance.

When to Use Videos

- **Educational Content**: Tutorials, demonstrations, or explainer videos.
- **Entertaining Content**: Short, engaging clips or storytelling.
- **Engaging Content**: Live streams or interactive videos.

Advantages

- Highly engaging and versatile.
- Effective for storytelling and emotional connections.
- Favored by algorithms on platforms like YouTube and TikTok.

2. Blogs

Blogs remain a cornerstone of long-form content, particularly for creators focusing on SEO and thought leadership.

When to Use Blogs

- **Educational Content**: In-depth how-to guides or case studies.

- **Engaging Content**: Discussion-driven posts with comment sections.

Advantages

- Evergreen potential with SEO optimization.
- Builds authority and credibility.
- Provides opportunities for monetization through ads and affiliate links.

---

3. Podcasts

Podcasts offer an intimate, long-form format ideal for discussions, storytelling, or deep dives into specific topics.

When to Use Podcasts

- **Educational Content**: Expert interviews or industry insights.
- **Entertaining Content**: Narrative-driven episodes or humor.
- **Engaging Content**: Q&A sessions or audience-submitted topics.

Advantages

- Encourages loyal and attentive listenership.
- Low production costs compared to video.
- Reaches audiences during commuting or multitasking.

---

4. Social Media Posts

Social media platforms (e.g., Instagram, Twitter, LinkedIn) excel at short-form, visually driven content.

When to Use Social Media Posts

- **Entertaining Content**: Memes, challenges, or relatable posts.
- **Engaging Content**: Polls, contests, and interactive stories.

Advantages

- Quick production and fast distribution.
- Ideal for reaching broad or niche audiences.
- Encourages interaction and virality.

Repurposing Content for Maximum Impact

Sun Tzu advises:

> "Exploit the enemy's weaknesses. Turn your disadvantage into advantage."

Repurposing content allows creators to maximize the value of their work by adapting it to different formats, platforms, and audiences. It ensures that a single piece of content can have multiple lives, reducing workload while increasing reach.

Benefits of Repurposing Content

1. **Efficiency**: Saves time and resources by reusing existing materials.
2. **Extended Reach**: Adapts content for diverse audiences and platforms.
3. **Consistency**: Reinforces key messages across multiple touchpoints.

How to Repurpose Content

1. **Transform Blogs into Videos**

    - Turn a written how-to guide into a tutorial video.
    - Use key points from an article as a script for YouTube or TikTok.
2. **Break Long Videos into Short Clips**

    - Extract highlight moments from a webinar or podcast and share as Instagram Reels or TikTok videos.
3. **Combine Social Media Posts into a Blog**

    - Use popular tweets or Instagram captions to build a comprehensive blog post.
4. **Create Infographics from Data**

    - Turn statistics or research findings into visually engaging infographics for Pinterest or Instagram.
5. **Compile User-Generated Content**

- Feature audience responses or submissions as standalone posts or part of a video.

Examples of Effective Repurposing

- A podcast episode discussing a trending topic could be transcribed into a blog, edited into a YouTube video, and summarized as a Twitter thread.
- A creator's live Q&A session could be recorded, clipped into short TikToks, and converted into an FAQ blog.

Sun Tzu's advice to "use the enemy's strength against them" applies to content repurposing—take what works in one format and adapt it for greater impact.

Conclusion

Content is the creator's most powerful weapon, but its effectiveness depends on how skillfully it is wielded. By understanding the different types of content, aligning formats with your strategy, and repurposing material for maximum reach, creators can build a robust and adaptable content arsenal.

Sun Tzu's timeless wisdom offers the perfect summary of this chapter:

> "The supreme art of war is to subdue the enemy without fighting."

In content creation, this means creating material so compelling, valuable, and engaging that it naturally captures attention and loyalty without the need for aggressive promotion. By mastering the art of content as a weapon, you position yourself for sustained success in an ever-changing digital battlefield.

Chapter 9: Building Alliances

In *The Art of War*, Sun Tzu speaks of the strategic advantages of alliances:

> "The clever combatant looks to the effect of combined energy, and does not require too much from individuals. Hence, his ability to pick out the right men and utilize combined energy."

This wisdom is as relevant for content creators as it was for ancient generals. Collaboration is a powerful tool for growth, allowing creators to pool resources, share audiences, and create value greater than the sum of their individual efforts. By forging alliances, creators can expand their reach, diversify their content, and strengthen their position in a competitive digital landscape.

This chapter explores the benefits of collaboration, effective networking strategies, and practical approaches like guest posts, co-productions, and partnerships.

Collaboration with Other Creators as a Force Multiplier

The Power of Combined Efforts

Collaboration enables creators to achieve outcomes that might be unattainable alone. Sun Tzu emphasizes the advantage of collective strength:

"An army may be likened to a stream of water, for just as flowing water avoids heights and hastens to the lowlands, so an army avoids strength and strikes weakness."

By collaborating with others, creators can compensate for their weaknesses and leverage the strengths of their allies. For instance:

- A skilled writer can partner with a talented videographer to produce a compelling video script.
- A creator with a small audience but niche expertise can collaborate with a broader-reaching creator to amplify their message.

Benefits of Collaboration

1. **Audience Growth**

   - Collaborating with another creator introduces your content to their audience, expanding your reach.
   - Sun Tzu writes, "The opportunity of defeating the enemy is provided by the enemy himself." Similarly, the opportunity to grow your audience often lies in alliances with creators whose followers might resonate with your message.

2. **Creative Synergy**

   - Partnerships foster fresh ideas and perspectives, leading to innovative content.

- For example, a fitness influencer and a nutritionist could co-create a series on holistic health.

3. **Shared Resources**

- Collaborations often involve sharing tools, skills, or platforms, reducing the individual workload and increasing the overall production quality.

4. **Increased Credibility**

- Partnering with a respected creator in your niche enhances your authority and builds trust with your audience.

Networking Strategies to Expand Your Reach

Networking is the foundation of collaboration. Sun Tzu advises:

> "Know your enemy and know yourself, and you can fight a hundred battles with no danger of defeat."

While in Sun Tzu's context, this involves understanding adversaries, for creators, the lesson applies to knowing and connecting with peers in the industry. Effective networking requires identifying potential collaborators, nurturing relationships, and creating mutual value.

---

1. Identify the Right Creators

Not all collaborations are equal. Successful partnerships align in values, audience demographics, and content goals. Look for creators who:

- Operate in complementary niches (e.g., a travel vlogger collaborating with a photography expert).
- Share your target audience but offer distinct expertise or style.
- Have a strong reputation for producing quality content.

---

2. Build Authentic Relationships

Sun Tzu emphasizes the importance of preparation:

> "The general who wins a battle makes many calculations in his temple before the battle is fought."

Building authentic relationships takes time and effort. Strategies include:

- **Engaging with Their Content**: Comment, like, and share their posts to show genuine interest.
- **Participating in Community Spaces**: Join forums, webinars, or live chats where creators in your niche congregate.
- **Reaching Out Thoughtfully**: When initiating contact, personalize your message and highlight shared interests or values.

3. Leverage Social Media and Networking Events

- **Social Media**: Platforms like LinkedIn, Instagram, and Twitter are excellent for connecting with creators. Use features like DMs or tagging to initiate conversations.
- **Events and Conferences**: Attend industry events, both virtual and in-person, to network with like-minded individuals.

4. Offer Value First

When approaching potential collaborators, focus on what you can bring to the table. Sun Tzu writes:

> "When you surround an army, leave an outlet free."

This principle underscores the importance of mutual benefit—your proposal should not feel one-sided but instead offer a clear advantage to your potential partner.

Guest Posts, Co-Productions, and Partnerships

Collaboration takes many forms, each with unique benefits and execution strategies. Sun Tzu's guidance to adapt strategies based on terrain applies here:

"He who knows the terrain and adapts his troops accordingly will always be victorious."

By selecting the right type of collaboration for your goals and circumstances, you maximize the chances of success.

Guest Posts

Guest posting involves creating content for another creator's platform, such as their blog, YouTube channel, or podcast. This approach allows you to reach a new audience while adding value to your collaborator's platform.

Benefits

- Introduces your expertise to a broader audience.
- Enhances your credibility by associating with established creators.
- Drives traffic back to your own platform through backlinks or mentions.

How to Succeed

- **Research Target Platforms**: Choose platforms whose audience aligns with your niche.
- **Pitch Compelling Ideas**: Tailor your pitch to the host's audience, focusing on unique and relevant topics.
- **Provide High-Quality Content**: Deliver well-researched, engaging content that adds value to the host platform.

Co-Productions

Co-productions involve collaborating on a single piece of content, such as a video, podcast, or social media post. This approach combines the strengths of both creators to produce something unique.

Examples

- A YouTube creator specializing in tech reviews partnering with a graphic designer to co-create a video on "The Best Tools for Creative Professionals."
- Two Instagram influencers hosting a joint live Q&A session.

Benefits

- Combines expertise and resources for higher-quality content.
- Allows cross-promotion on multiple platforms.
- Builds a stronger relationship between collaborators.

How to Succeed

- **Define Roles Clearly**: Agree on who will handle which aspects of production, from scripting to editing.
- **Align on Goals**: Ensure both creators share a common vision for the project.
- **Promote Collaboratively**: Plan joint promotion strategies to maximize reach.

Partnerships

Partnerships involve longer-term collaborations, such as co-hosting a podcast, launching a product together, or creating a content series.

Examples

- A fitness creator partnering with a brand to launch a line of workout gear.
- A travel vlogger teaming up with a tourism board to create a multi-episode destination guide.

Benefits

- Provides consistent opportunities for collaboration.
- Builds deeper connections between collaborators and their audiences.
- Opens new revenue streams or growth opportunities.

How to Succeed

- **Formalize Agreements**: Clearly outline roles, revenue splits, and expectations in writing.
- **Communicate Regularly**: Maintain open communication to address challenges and ensure alignment.
- **Evolve the Partnership**: Adapt the collaboration over time to keep it fresh and relevant.

Case Studies: Successful Collaborations

1. YouTube: Smosh and Anthony Padilla

The comedy channel Smosh collaborated with other creators like Anthony Padilla, leveraging combined audiences to create viral content. This partnership allowed Smosh to grow its subscriber base while diversifying its offerings.

---

2. Instagram: Content Creators and Brands

Influencers like Chiara Ferragni built their platforms by partnering with fashion brands for campaigns. These collaborations were mutually beneficial, with brands gaining exposure and creators enhancing their credibility.

---

3. Podcasts: Dax Shepard and Guest Co-Hosts

The *Armchair Expert* podcast thrives on collaborations with guest co-hosts, who bring fresh perspectives and attract new listeners. Each episode expands Shepard's reach while offering valuable insights to his audience.

Conclusion

Building alliances through collaboration is one of the most powerful strategies for content creators. Sun Tzu's wisdom about the strength of combined efforts applies directly:

> "The power of an army lies in its unity."

By partnering with other creators, leveraging networking strategies, and exploring collaborative formats like guest posts and co-productions, creators can multiply their impact and achieve their goals more effectively. Strategic alliances are not just a path to growth—they are a cornerstone of sustained success in the ever-evolving digital landscape.

Chapter 10: The Algorithmic Battlefield

In *The Art of War*, Sun Tzu reminds us:

> "If you know the enemy and know yourself, you need
> not fear the result of a hundred battles."

In the realm of content creation, the "enemy" is not a hostile army but the ever-changing algorithms that govern visibility and engagement on digital platforms. Algorithms are the unseen forces shaping how content is distributed, discovered, and consumed. They determine whether a post goes viral or sinks into obscurity.

To thrive in this algorithmic battlefield, creators must not only understand how algorithms work but also learn to adapt and mitigate risks associated with sudden changes. This chapter delves into the intricacies of algorithms, strategies to stay visible and engaging, and ways to safeguard your content strategy against unpredictable shifts.

Understanding and Leveraging Algorithms to Your Advantage

Algorithms are the rules and processes platforms use to deliver content to users. Sun Tzu's advice on knowing the terrain applies here:

> "Know the terrain and the weather, and your victory
> will not be impeded."

Understanding how algorithms prioritize content allows creators to tailor their strategies for maximum reach and engagement.

How Algorithms Work

While each platform has unique algorithms, most prioritize content based on the following factors:

1. **Relevance**: Content that matches user interests or recent interactions.
2. **Engagement**: Posts with higher likes, shares, comments, or watch time are more likely to be promoted.
3. **Timeliness**: Recent content often takes precedence over older posts.
4. **Consistency**: Regular posting signals to the algorithm that a creator is active and reliable.
5. **Quality**: Content that keeps users on the platform longer is rewarded, whether through detailed blogs, engaging videos, or interactive posts.

Leveraging Algorithms

Sun Tzu writes:

> "Take advantage of the enemy's unpreparedness;
> travel by unexpected routes and strike where he has
> taken no precautions."

For creators, this means exploiting algorithmic preferences to maximize reach.

1. Create Engaging Content

Platforms prioritize engagement as a key metric. Focus on creating material that encourages likes, comments, shares, and clicks. Strategies include:

- **Asking Questions**: End posts with a question to spark conversation.
- **Encouraging Interaction**: Use polls, quizzes, or challenges to engage followers.
- **Replying to Comments**: Engaging with your audience boosts the post's visibility.

2. Optimize Timing

Understanding when your audience is most active ensures your content gets maximum exposure. Use platform insights to determine peak times and schedule your posts accordingly.

3. Use Keywords and Hashtags

SEO principles apply to algorithms:

- On platforms like YouTube and Pinterest, use keywords in titles, descriptions, and tags to improve discoverability.
- On Instagram and TikTok, use relevant hashtags to reach broader audiences.

4. Experiment with Formats

Newer formats often receive algorithmic boosts as platforms promote their adoption. For example:

- Instagram prioritized Reels after their launch to compete with TikTok.
- YouTube shorts gained significant visibility due to their alignment with trending short-form content.

Tips for Staying Visible and Engaging on Platforms

Remaining visible in an algorithm-driven world requires proactive strategies. Sun Tzu's emphasis on adaptability is crucial:

> "In the midst of chaos, there is also opportunity."

Here's how to stay consistently visible and engaging across platforms:

1. Post Consistently

Algorithms reward creators who post regularly. Consistency signals reliability and keeps your audience engaged. Develop a content calendar to maintain a steady posting schedule.

---

2. Prioritize High-Quality Content

Quality is as important as quantity. Platforms like YouTube and LinkedIn prioritize content that provides value, whether through education, entertainment, or inspiration. Consider Sun Tzu's advice:

> "The victorious army is the one whose preparation is
> superior."

Focus on producing polished, meaningful content that aligns with
your brand and audience needs.

---

3. Engage with Your Audience

Platforms reward two-way communication. Strategies include:

- **Replying to Comments**: Builds community and boosts
  engagement.
- **Live Interactions**: Platforms like Instagram Live or
  YouTube Live often prioritize live streams in feeds.
- **User-Generated Content**: Encourage followers to create
  content around your brand and engage with their posts.

---

4. Analyze and Iterate

Use platform analytics to track the performance of your posts. Sun
Tzu writes:

> "Ponder and deliberate before you make a move."

Analyze what works and refine your strategy accordingly:

- Identify the type of content that generates the most
  engagement.
- Adjust your posting times based on audience activity.

- Test new formats to see how they perform.

---

5. Diversify Your Content

Algorithms often favor diverse content. Mix up your approach:

- **Videos**: Tutorials, vlogs, or short clips.
- **Static Posts**: Infographics, quotes, or photos.
- **Stories**: Behind-the-scenes glimpses or quick updates.
- **Interactive Elements**: Polls, quizzes, and questions.

Mitigating Risks of Algorithm Changes

Sun Tzu cautions against complacency:

> "Do not repeat the tactics which have gained you one victory, but let your methods be regulated by the infinite variety of circumstances."

Algorithm changes are inevitable and can dramatically impact visibility. Mitigating these risks requires preparation and adaptability.

1. Build an Owned Audience

One of the biggest risks of relying on algorithms is losing access to your audience if a platform's rules change. Build an owned audience by:

- Creating an email list to maintain direct communication.
- Encouraging followers to subscribe to multiple platforms.
- Developing a website or blog as a central hub for your content.

2. Stay Updated

Follow platform announcements and industry news to stay ahead of changes. Tools like Social Media Examiner or newsletters from platforms provide insights into updates and trends.

3. Diversify Platforms

Relying on a single platform increases vulnerability. Sun Tzu's emphasis on flexibility applies:

> "Be extremely subtle, even to the point of formlessness."

Expand your presence across multiple platforms to reduce dependence on any one algorithm. For example:

- A YouTuber could also maintain an Instagram account and a blog.
- A TikTok creator could repurpose videos for YouTube Shorts or Instagram Reels.

4. Focus on Evergreen Content

Trendy content may gain short-term visibility, but evergreen content provides long-lasting value. Examples include:

- How-to guides.
- Timeless advice in your niche.
- High-quality, searchable videos on YouTube.

---

5. Foster Community

Algorithms may change, but a loyal audience ensures consistent engagement. Focus on building genuine connections:

- Create a community space, like a Facebook group or Discord server.
- Engage directly with followers through polls, comments, and live sessions.

Case Study: Navigating Algorithm Shifts

Instagram Algorithm Changes

In 2016, Instagram switched from a chronological feed to an engagement-based algorithm. Many creators saw declines in visibility and engagement. Successful creators adapted by:

- Posting at times when their followers were most active.
- Creating more engaging captions to encourage comments.
- Using Instagram Stories to stay visible in followers' feeds.

YouTube's Emphasis on Watch Time

YouTube's algorithm update prioritized watch time over views. Creators who adapted by producing longer, engaging videos (e.g., tutorials, deep dives) saw significant growth, while those relying on short, clickbait content struggled.

Conclusion

Navigating the algorithmic battlefield requires a mix of strategy, adaptability, and resilience. By understanding how algorithms work, leveraging tools to maximize visibility, and preparing for inevitable changes, creators can maintain their momentum in an ever-evolving landscape.

Sun Tzu's wisdom encapsulates the essence of this chapter:

> "Victory belongs to the most persevering."

For content creators, the ability to persevere amidst shifting algorithms and emerging trends is key to long-term success. By staying proactive, diversifying platforms, and focusing on

meaningful engagement, you can thrive in the algorithmic
battlefield and maintain a strong connection with your audience.

Chapter 11: Discipline and Consistency

Sun Tzu writes in *The Art of War*:

> "Victory is the reward of discipline and strategic foresight."

In the realm of content creation, discipline and consistency are indispensable. They are the backbone of long-term success, separating fleeting creators from those who build lasting impact. While talent and creativity are essential, discipline ensures that creativity becomes action, and consistency ensures that action becomes habit.

This chapter delves into the importance of discipline in content creation, the process of building effective habits and routines, and tools to avoid burnout while maintaining creativity.

The Role of Discipline in Achieving Long-Term Success

Discipline as the Foundation of Success

Discipline is the ability to stay committed to a goal regardless of challenges, distractions, or fluctuations in motivation. Sun Tzu emphasizes the importance of steadfast preparation:

"He will win who, prepared himself, waits to take the enemy unprepared."

For creators, discipline is the engine that drives progress, even on days when inspiration wanes. The digital landscape rewards those who show up consistently, building trust and anticipation with their audience. Whether you're a blogger, YouTuber, or social media influencer, discipline ensures that your content continues to flow, meeting both algorithmic demands and audience expectations.

The Long-Term Benefits of Discipline

1. **Audience Trust** Consistent posting builds reliability, making audiences more likely to return. A disciplined creator becomes a trusted presence in their audience's lives, similar to a favorite show airing weekly.

2. **Cumulative Growth** Just as Sun Tzu speaks of gaining advantage through careful planning, disciplined creators see their efforts compound over time. Regular posts, even small ones, contribute to significant growth.

3. **Resilience** Discipline allows creators to push through difficult periods, such as algorithm changes or temporary engagement drops. Sun Tzu advises:

"The wise warrior prepares for every contingency."

By sticking to a plan, creators are better equipped to weather setbacks and keep progressing.

Building Habits and Routines for Consistent Content Creation

Habits and routines form the bedrock of discipline. Sun Tzu's focus on preparation applies here:

> "The quality of decision is like the well-timed swoop of a falcon which enables it to strike and destroy its victim."

By building intentional routines, creators streamline decision-making and maximize productivity.

Steps to Build Habits for Consistency

1. **Define Clear Goals** Start with specific, measurable goals for your content. For example:

   - Publish one blog post every week.
   - Upload two YouTube videos per month.
   - Post daily updates on Instagram.
2. Clear goals provide a roadmap, making it easier to establish routines.

2. **Create a Content Calendar** A content calendar serves as a strategic plan for your publishing schedule. Sun Tzu emphasizes:

"Victorious warriors win first and then go to war."

Plan your content topics, formats, and deadlines in advance to reduce uncertainty and maintain focus.

---

3. **Schedule Dedicated Time for Creation** Treat content creation like any other professional commitment. Dedicate specific hours each day or week to brainstorming, producing, and editing content. For example:

    o Use mornings for ideation and writing.
    o Allocate afternoons for filming or editing videos.
4. Sun Tzu's guidance on timing resonates here:

"Every battle is won or lost before it is fought."

Scheduling ensures you prioritize content creation before distractions arise.

4. **Start Small and Scale Up** Building habits takes time.
    Begin with manageable goals, such as posting twice a
    week, and gradually increase your output as the routine
    becomes ingrained.

    Sun Tzu writes:

    "The journey of a thousand miles begins with a single
    step."

    Small, consistent efforts lead to sustainable long-term
    growth.

5. **Track Progress and Adjust** Regularly assess your
    performance and adapt your habits. Use tools like analytics
    dashboards to evaluate which routines are working and
    where improvements are needed.

Tools to Avoid Burnout and Maintain Creativity

While discipline and consistency are crucial, they must be
balanced with strategies to prevent burnout. Sun Tzu advises:

"Do not press an enemy at bay."

Overworking yourself without periods of rest can lead to mental and creative fatigue, ultimately harming your content quality and personal well-being.

---

1. Establish Boundaries

- Set clear boundaries between work and personal life. For example:

    - Dedicate specific hours to work and unplug after.
    - Avoid checking analytics obsessively outside of work hours.
- Sun Tzu reminds us:

    "Control your troops as you would your own children."

    Take care of yourself as a critical component of your creative "army."

---

2. Use Productivity Tools

Leverage tools to streamline your workflow and reduce stress:

- **Project Management**: Use platforms like Trello or Notion to organize tasks and track progress.
- **Scheduling Software**: Tools like Buffer or Later automate post scheduling, freeing up time for creativity.
- **Content Templates**: Create reusable templates for blog layouts, video intros, or social media graphics to save time.

3. Embrace Downtime

Allow yourself time to recharge. Sun Tzu advises:

> "Opportunities multiply as they are seized."

Rest and relaxation provide the clarity and energy needed to recognize and seize new opportunities.

4. Collaborate

Collaboration reduces workload and introduces fresh perspectives. Partnering with other creators can relieve the pressure of constantly ideating and executing alone.

5. Prioritize Self-Care

Maintaining physical and mental health is essential for creativity. Sun Tzu notes:

"The skillful fighter avoids fatigue."

Incorporate self-care practices, such as:

- Regular exercise.
- Mindfulness or meditation.
- Adequate sleep and nutrition.

---

6. Find Inspiration

Creativity flourishes when inspired. Surround yourself with diverse influences—books, music, art, or nature—and take breaks to explore new ideas.

Case Studies of Discipline and Consistency

1. Casey Neistat's Daily Vlogging

Casey Neistat became a YouTube sensation by committing to daily vlogging for over a year. His disciplined routine not only grew his audience exponentially but also refined his storytelling skills.

Key Lesson: Consistency builds momentum and keeps audiences engaged.

---

2. Seth Godin's Daily Blog

Marketing guru Seth Godin has published a blog post daily for over a decade. His unwavering discipline has made him a thought leader and an inspiration to countless entrepreneurs.

Key Lesson: Long-term consistency establishes authority and credibility.

---

3. Marie Forleo's Weekly Videos

Marie Forleo built her brand by releasing high-quality weekly videos on entrepreneurship and personal development. Her disciplined approach ensured her audience could rely on her for regular value-packed content.

Key Lesson: Predictable routines create anticipation and loyalty.

Conclusion

Discipline and consistency are the twin pillars of sustained success in content creation. By cultivating habits, establishing routines, and leveraging tools to maintain creativity, creators can achieve their long-term goals while avoiding burnout. Sun Tzu's wisdom encapsulates the essence of this chapter:

> "He who is prudent and lies in wait for an enemy who is not, will be victorious."

In the algorithm-driven world of digital content, prudence and preparation are the keys to standing out. By embracing discipline and consistency, creators not only build their audience but also fortify themselves against the challenges of an ever-evolving landscape.

Chapter 12: Measuring Success

Sun Tzu writes in *The Art of War*:

> "Victorious warriors win first and then go to war, while defeated warriors go to war first and then seek to win."

This principle underscores the importance of preparation, observation, and learning from the battlefield—critical elements for any content creator aiming to succeed. Measuring success in the digital world involves understanding key metrics, evaluating the effectiveness of your strategy, and continuously iterating based on data. Without clear measurement, creators risk wasting resources on efforts that fail to connect or resonate with their audience.

This chapter explores the key metrics to track, how to evaluate strategy effectiveness, and actionable steps to refine your approach using data.

Key Metrics to Track for Content Creators

Understanding which metrics matter is the first step in measuring success. Sun Tzu emphasizes the importance of knowing both the terrain and the enemy:

> "The general who wins a battle makes many calculations in his temple before the battle is fought."

For creators, the "calculations" involve analyzing metrics that align with their goals.

---

1. Engagement Metrics

Engagement reflects how well your audience connects with your content. It is one of the most critical indicators of success across platforms.

Key Engagement Metrics

- **Likes and Reactions**: Measure audience approval or interest.
- **Comments**: Indicate deeper interaction and investment in your content.
- **Shares**: Highlight how shareable and valuable your content is to your audience.
- **Click-Through Rates (CTR)**: Show how effectively your content drives traffic to external links or additional content.

Engagement metrics signal the quality of your content and how effectively it resonates with your audience. Sun Tzu's focus on the dynamics of strength applies here:

"Opportunities multiply as they are seized."

Strong engagement fosters visibility and further opportunities for growth.

---

2. Reach and Impressions

Reach measures how many unique users see your content, while impressions count how often your content is displayed. These metrics help gauge your visibility and the size of your audience.

Key Reach Metrics

- **Follower Growth**: Tracks the increase or decrease in your audience size.
- **Viral Reach**: Measures the audience gained through shares, tags, or trends.
- **Impressions vs. Reach**: Understanding the ratio helps identify whether content is being shown repeatedly to the same users.

3. Website and Blog Metrics

For creators with blogs or websites, understanding site performance is essential.

Key Website Metrics

- **Traffic**: Tracks the number of visitors over time.
- **Bounce Rate**: Measures how often users leave without engaging further.
- **Time on Page**: Indicates how engaging your content is.
- **Conversion Rate**: Tracks how many users take desired actions (e.g., subscribing to a newsletter or purchasing a product).

4. Video Performance Metrics

On video platforms like YouTube or TikTok, understanding video performance is crucial.

Key Video Metrics

- **Watch Time**: Measures the total time users spend watching your videos.
- **Retention Rate**: Tracks how much of the video is watched before viewers drop off.
- **Subscribers Gained**: Indicates how well your videos attract new followers.
- **Engagement on Video**: Includes likes, comments, and shares specific to video content.

---

5. Revenue Metrics

For creators monetizing their content, tracking revenue-related metrics is vital.

Key Revenue Metrics

- **Ad Revenue**: Earnings from ads displayed on your content.
- **Affiliate Sales**: Revenue generated from affiliate links.
- **Product Sales**: Income from merchandise, courses, or services.
- **Return on Investment (ROI)**: Measures the financial success of campaigns relative to costs.

How to Evaluate the Effectiveness of Your Strategy

Sun Tzu reminds us:

> "The enlightened ruler lays his plans well ahead; the good general cultivates his resources."

Evaluating your strategy involves connecting your goals with measurable outcomes, identifying strengths, and addressing weaknesses.

---

1. Set Clear Objectives

Start by aligning your metrics with your overarching goals. For example:

- **Goal: Build a Community**
  - Metrics: Engagement rates, comments, and shares.
- **Goal: Drive Website Traffic**
  - Metrics: Click-through rates, referral traffic, and bounce rates.
- **Goal: Generate Revenue**
  - Metrics: Conversion rates, ad revenue, and ROI.

Sun Tzu's advice on planning applies:

> "The general who wins makes calculations before the battle."

Having clear objectives ensures you measure what matters most.

---

2. Analyze Trends Over Time

Evaluate data over weeks or months to identify trends and patterns. Look for:

- Content types or formats that consistently perform well.
- Seasonal or time-based spikes in engagement.
- Metrics that show steady growth versus those that stagnate.

3. Compare Performance Across Platforms

If you operate on multiple platforms (e.g., Instagram, TikTok, YouTube), compare performance to identify where your efforts yield the greatest results. For instance:

- Does short-form content perform better than long-form?
- Which platform drives the most traffic to your website?

Sun Tzu emphasizes understanding the terrain:

> "He who knows the terrain and the weather will win."

By understanding which platforms best suit your content, you can allocate resources strategically.

---

4. Assess Audience Feedback

Quantitative metrics provide numbers, but qualitative feedback adds depth. Analyze comments, direct messages, and survey responses to understand your audience's thoughts and preferences.

Iterating and Improving Based on Data

Sun Tzu states:

> "Ponder and deliberate before you make a move."

Data should not only inform you but guide the evolution of your strategy. Continuous improvement ensures you remain relevant, efficient, and impactful.

1. Identify High-Performing Content

Analyze your top-performing posts to identify what resonates. Consider:

- Topics: Which themes or niches attract the most engagement?
- Format: Does your audience prefer videos, blogs, or infographics?
- Timing: When is your audience most active?

Use this information to replicate success while experimenting with similar content.

2. Address Weaknesses

Look at underperforming content to identify areas for improvement:

- Are your headlines or thumbnails unappealing?
- Is the content too generic or misaligned with your audience's needs?

Sun Tzu reminds us:

"In the midst of chaos, there is also opportunity."

Weaknesses often point to opportunities for refinement and growth.

---

3. Experiment with New Strategies

Use data to justify calculated risks. For example:

- If short videos perform well, experiment with TikTok or Instagram Reels.
- If your audience prefers personal stories, incorporate more storytelling into your blogs or posts.

---

4. Set Incremental Goals

Break your long-term objectives into smaller milestones based on past performance. For instance:

- If your engagement rate is 10%, aim for a 12% increase in the next quarter.
- If you gain 100 followers per month, set a goal to reach 150.

5. Automate and Streamline

Sun Tzu advises:

> "Move not unless you see an advantage."

Focus on efficiency by automating repetitive tasks, such as:

- Scheduling posts using tools like Buffer or Hootsuite.
- Using analytics platforms like Google Analytics or YouTube Studio for real-time performance insights.

Case Studies: Measuring Success

1. YouTube Creator: Peter McKinnon

Peter McKinnon, a photography and videography creator, used data to refine his content strategy. By analyzing watch time and retention, he focused on creating visually captivating tutorials, boosting his audience engagement and growth.

2. Instagram Influencer: Jenna Kutcher

Jenna Kutcher measured success by analyzing engagement metrics on Instagram. She shifted from generic posts to personal stories and value-driven captions, significantly increasing audience interaction.

3. Blogger: Neil Patel

Neil Patel tracks metrics like organic traffic, bounce rates, and conversions on his blog. By iterating based on data, he optimized SEO and provided tailored content, maintaining his position as a leading voice in digital marketing.

Conclusion

Measuring success is not a one-time task but an ongoing process of analysis, adaptation, and improvement. By tracking the right metrics, evaluating strategy effectiveness, and iterating based on data, creators can ensure they remain aligned with their goals while staying responsive to audience needs.

Sun Tzu's wisdom encapsulates the essence of this chapter:

> "What the ancients called a clever fighter is one who
> not only wins but excels in winning with ease."

For content creators, excellence lies in using data to craft strategies that consistently deliver results, transforming effort into sustainable success. By mastering the art of measurement and iteration, you position yourself not just to survive but to thrive in the ever-changing digital battlefield.

Conclusion: The Journey Ahead

In *The Art of War*, Sun Tzu writes:

> "Strategy without tactics is the slowest route to victory.
> Tactics without strategy is the noise before defeat."

These words resonate deeply with content creators, whose success hinges on the delicate balance of vision and execution. The journey through this book has mapped the intricate parallels between Sun Tzu's timeless principles of warfare and the modern art of content creation. Now, as we stand at the edge of the battlefield, it is time to reflect, adapt, and charge forward with purpose.

Revisiting the Parallels Between *The Art of War* and Content Creation

1. Strategy as the Backbone

Sun Tzu begins his work by emphasizing the importance of preparation:

> "The art of war is of vital importance to the state."

In the realm of content creation, strategy forms the backbone of success. Whether it's defining your niche, understanding your audience, or crafting a long-term vision, preparation determines whether your efforts will flourish or falter. Just as generals must understand the terrain and their opponents, creators must grasp the intricacies of their platforms, competitors, and audience preferences.

---

2. Adaptability as a Survival Skill

The ever-changing nature of digital platforms mirrors the unpredictability of the battlefield. Sun Tzu advises:

> "In the midst of chaos, there is also opportunity."

Creators must embrace adaptability as a core competency. From pivoting strategies in response to algorithm changes to experimenting with emerging trends, success demands a willingness to evolve. The ability to see opportunities in the midst of uncertainty is what separates the resilient from the overwhelmed.

---

3. Consistency as a Weapon

Sun Tzu's wisdom on discipline resonates powerfully in content creation:

> "Disorder comes from order, fear comes from courage, weakness comes from strength."

Consistency is the key to building trust, reliability, and growth. Whether it's a steady posting schedule or a recognizable voice, disciplined creators build momentum over time, fostering relationships with their audience and staying top of mind in a crowded marketplace.

---

4. Collaboration as a Force Multiplier

Alliances are vital in both war and content creation. Sun Tzu writes:

> "The clever combatant looks to the effect of combined energy, and does not require too much from individuals."

Collaborating with other creators, brands, or communities amplifies your reach and creates synergies that lead to exponential growth. Partnerships unlock potential beyond what a single creator can achieve alone, driving innovation and deeper connections with diverse audiences.

---

5. Metrics as Intelligence

No battle is fought blindly, and no content strategy should proceed without data. Sun Tzu's emphasis on knowing your enemy and terrain aligns with the importance of analytics in content creation:

> "If you know the enemy and know yourself, you need not fear the result of a hundred battles."

Tracking metrics, analyzing performance, and iterating based on data ensure that your strategies remain effective and aligned with your goals.

Encouragement for Creators to Stay Strategic and Adaptable

The digital world is a vast, dynamic battlefield. Trends shift overnight, algorithms evolve without warning, and audience expectations continually grow. Yet, as Sun Tzu reminds us:

> "The wise warrior avoids the battle that cannot be won."

The path of a content creator is not about fighting every battle but about choosing the right ones. Staying strategic and adaptable allows you to focus your energy on efforts that yield the greatest impact. Here are key encouragements to carry forward:

1. Trust the Process

Growth in content creation is rarely linear. There will be setbacks, challenges, and moments of doubt. Sun Tzu advises patience:

> "The wheels of justice grind slowly, but they grind exceedingly fine."

Every effort contributes to your journey, even if the results are not immediately visible. Trust that consistency and strategy will yield success over time.

2. Embrace Change

Change is not the enemy; it is the catalyst for innovation. Sun Tzu writes:

> "Water shapes its course according to the nature of the ground over which it flows."

Just as water adapts to its terrain, creators must adapt to new platforms, audience preferences, and technological advancements. View change as an opportunity to grow, learn, and innovate.

---

3. Focus on Connection

Amid the pursuit of metrics and growth, never lose sight of the human element. Your audience is not a number but a community of individuals seeking connection, inspiration, or solutions. Sun Tzu reminds us:

> "Treat your men as you would your own beloved sons, and they will follow you into the deepest valley."

By prioritizing authenticity, empathy, and value, you build relationships that transcend trends and algorithms.

Final Call to Action: Implementing the Lessons Learned

This journey through the principles of *The Art of War* has equipped you with tools, strategies, and mindsets to thrive as a content creator. But knowledge alone is not enough—action is the ultimate differentiator. Sun Tzu declares:

> "A journey of a thousand miles begins with a single step."

Here is your final call to action:

---

1. Revisit Your Mission

Start by reaffirming your purpose as a creator. What message do you want to share? Who is your ideal audience? How do you want to impact their lives? A clear mission serves as your compass, guiding every decision and action.

---

2. Craft a Strategic Plan

Build a content calendar that aligns with your goals. Define your long-term vision, break it into actionable steps, and schedule your efforts. Sun Tzu writes:

> "Plan for what is difficult while it is easy, do what is great while it is small."

Begin with manageable tasks and scale up as you build momentum.

---

3. Experiment and Adapt

Test new formats, platforms, and strategies to discover what resonates with your audience. Treat failures as valuable feedback, refining your approach with each iteration. Sun Tzu's advice to generals applies here:

> "Victory comes from finding opportunities in problems."

---

4. Measure and Reflect

Track your progress with the key metrics outlined in Chapter 12. Regularly evaluate your strategy's effectiveness and make data-driven adjustments. Reflection ensures that your efforts remain aligned with your evolving goals.

---

5. Build Meaningful Connections

Seek collaborations, engage with your audience, and nurture relationships within your community. Remember Sun Tzu's insight:

> "Unity leads to strength."

By fostering alliances and partnerships, you amplify your reach and create enduring impact.

---

6. Stay Resilient

The journey of a content creator is not without its challenges. Engagement might dip, algorithms might shift, and doubts might creep in. Yet, Sun Tzu reminds us:

> "He who is prudent and lies in wait for an enemy who is not, will be victorious."

Perseverance, coupled with strategy, is your greatest ally.

The Final Word

Content creation is both an art and a battle, requiring creativity, strategy, and resilience. The lessons of *The Art of War* serve as a timeless guide, offering creators a framework to navigate the complexities of the digital landscape. As you step forward, armed with knowledge and determination, remember that your journey is unique, and success is not just about winning battles but about staying true to your vision.

Sun Tzu's final encouragement resonates as a closing thought:

> "In the midst of chaos, there is also opportunity."

Go forth boldly, seize the opportunities before you, and craft a legacy that inspires, connects, and endures. The battlefield awaits, and your story is yet to be written.

THIS IS NOT A COLLECTION

This volume is part of **Ancient Wisdom Hacks—**
an ongoing body of work focused on how strategy, power, and
failure actually function under pressure.

The books are only one layer.

What you are reading is an entry point into a larger system of
interpretation, application, and expansion.

WHAT THESE WORKS ARE DESIGNED TO DO

Most people look for answers.

These works expose patterns:

- How decisions are made before they are visible
- How systems weaken before they collapse
- How power shifts before it is recognized

This is not theory.
It is applied observation.

THE SYSTEM BEHIND THE WORK

Across all volumes and future releases, three forces remain
constant:

- **Strategy** — how outcomes are shaped before action
- **Conflict** — how people and systems break under pressure
- **Power** — how control is gained, maintained, and lost

No single book contains the full picture.
Each adds another angle.

CONTINUE BEYOND THIS VOLUME

New interpretations, applied volumes, and extended works are released continuously.

To access current and future material, visit:

www.AncientWisdomHacks.com

WHAT YOU WILL FIND

- Additional applied volumes across industries
- Expanded interpretations of foundational texts
- New releases not available through standard distribution
- Future projects extending beyond books

The system is still expanding.

FINAL POSITION

Clarity does not make outcomes easier.

It removes the illusion that they were ever simple.

Ancient Wisdom Hacks
Interpretation over repetition.
Application over theory.